Got Homophobia?

By Azaan Kamau

for
donnie
dijan
bruttus

Got Homophobia?

By Azaan Kamau

Acknowledgements

First I would like to my Divine Creator, because if it weren't for my relationship with you, my understanding of the teachings, belief in my prayers, and continued unwavering faith, I just can't imagine where I would be. Thank you Lord!

Thank you so very much to my beloved Brother Donnie Dijan Bruttus for loving me unconditionally, reading me poetry and loving me no matter what! Thank you! I love you Dijan!

Thank you to my grandparents Louella & Willis for love, guidance, and empowerment. Because of you, I AM.

THANK YOU, THANK YOU, THANK YOU to my Ancestors, my warriors, griots, healers, mentors, prayer ministries, spiritual family, siblings and friends. Mad, mad props to Tara J. Brown who guides me with her actions, her dignity, and reverence. The legendary infamous Ifalade Ta'Shia Asanti who has truly mothered and molded me, I love you Pops; Debra "Pepper" Massey, My African advisor Eva Georgia, The soulja Salima MaSud, The one and only Linda Hobbs who keeps me focused and alert, The true pioneer in SGL/LGBT/ GBF media, publishing, poetry, literature, marketing and independent film...Stephanie "Dakara" Wynn; YOU ARE AMAZING! Angela Odom for fighting and marching like a warrior! Tammy Young whose unrelenting support has paved the way for many works of art, publications, and programs. The true Visionary Michael Beckwith, The mastermind Jeffrey King, Terry Lynn Howcott, the glue that binds! The literary shaman Katrina Arango for igniting the publishing fire! The one who forged forward no matter what; Bonnie Henderson, Angel Tyree who said, "Do The Dayuuumed Thang Azaan!"

Greg Mc Neal, my artistic amazing bratha...Please know our many conversations and your friendship mean the world to me.

To my siblings, and cousins...I thank you! Mario D. Coleman, thank you for guiding me to the Nxl Lvl!

It would behoove me not to thank everyone who ever called me boy, it, dyke, bull-dagger, she-man, mack truck, bull in a China cabinet, lezzie, mighty-macha, bull-dyke, lesbo, dykey, and a bunch other things that made my skin crawl! Thank you!

Copyright © 2010 by Glover Lane Press

Glover Lane Press
4570 Van Nuys Blvd Suite 573
Sherman Oaks, Ca 91403

No part of this book may be reproduced,
Stored in a retrieval system,
or transmitted by any means, electronic or
mechanical without the written permission of
Azaan Kamau

First Published by Glover lane Press
 October 2010
Jennifer Glover C/O Glover Lane Press
gloverpublishing@gmail.com or
azaankamau@gmail.com
http://lulu.com/spotlight/azaankamau
http://blurb.com/user/store/Azaankamau

Other Titles By Glover Lane Press/ Azaan Kamau Media

The Memoirs of Madlyn F. Glover;
Love & Romance with Ray Charles Robinson
STUD; Dispelling The Myths
In The Midst of My Blackness
Riveting
A Z A A N; Behind The Lens
ROOTS; A Charleston Plantation
KATRINA; Turbulent Waters
The Dank Dictionary
The Cannabis Epicurean

If We Must Die

If we must die, let it not be like hogs

Hunted and penned in an inglorious spot,

While round us bark the mad and hungry dogs,

Making their mock at our accursed lot.

If we must die, O let us nobly die

So that our precious blood may not be shed

In vain; then even the monsters we defy

Shall be constrained to honor us though dead!

O kinsmen! We must meet the common foe!

Though far outnumbered let us show us brave,

And for their thousand blows deal one death blow!

What though before us lies the open grave?

Like men we'll face the murderous, cowardly pack,

Pressed to the wall, dying, but fighting back!

Author, Claude McKay

The Table of Contents

Introduction	9
Homophobia & Heterosexism. What is it?	21
African American Historical Viewpoint	29
Faith Based War Against Gay Rights	32
Black Men, Homophobia & The Down Low	34
Men of the Cloth as Sexual Predators, Perverts & Child Molesters	37
HIV/AIDS & The Church	39
Dr. Martin Luther King & Coretta Scott King Felt…	44
A Parent's Role	47
Homophobia, Bullying & Suicide Prevention	50
Tools to fight the Ignorance	53
The Bottom Line	55
VICTIMS OF HOMOPHOBIA, BULLYING AND CRIMES OF HATE	56
Resources for SGL/ LGBT Communities	67
About The Author	68

INTRODUCTION

At a very young age, some of my earliest memories are of the slurs bull-dagger, punk, and sissy. I just could not understand if these people were happy, (gay) and they loved everyone, why were they so hated?

I learned that homophobia was a curable ignorance that cut me to the bone. As a black female, I was taught what role I must play, what box to fit in, what lines not to cross, how to stay in the straight line and know my place as a female. And most important be a lady so that I can get and keep a man! I wasn't feminine or dainty. I didn't want to play jax, hop scotch or jump rope! I loathed my big pink skinned plastic baby dolls. I felt offended, humiliated and even insulted.
Of course I leaped from the box of African American female conformity, refused to submit! I was more interested in how airplanes stayed in the sky, how the piano keys made sound and my fascination with animals. I just wanted to play with my dog Peanut, my toy motorcycle collection or one of my many 1964 Impala Hot Wheels!

They called me a tomboy and insisted I would grow out of it. When adolescence hit, I was very physical and aggressive with everything I did. I wanted to climb trees, race cars...I wanted to slam dunk! I wore fedoras, suits and square toed shoes! I felt happy and affirmed until 'bull-dyke' and or other slurs slapped me and wounded me to my core! Homophobia was close at hand!

I grew up being pulled between superstitious tradition and spiritual truths. Many in my family, opposed my liberal grandparents because of how they reared me. My grandmother gave me sound, strict education, structure, discipline and unconditional love. She gave me the courage to just be myself and never to allow words to hurt me. Along with that rearing came many lessons about racism, homophobia, art, culture, religion, etc. My grandfather taught me to be a warrior! He said, "We should walk in the footprints of our ancestors, and soldiers are led, and warriors are chosen." He taught me that, if I had knowledge, I had the ultimate power that no one could ever take from me.

My grandparents instilled in me the wisdom to see Spirit in ALL living things. They taught me to have reverence for everything from blades of grass to the crippled and ostracized. I honor my African and Choctaw heritage in the traditional way taught to me by them. They taught me how to articulate my thoughts and feelings. Throughout my life Blacks have said, "you talk is like white folk!"

My Grandmother would simply say, "You speak the language of W.E.B. Dubois, Fredrick Douglas, Langston Hughes and Martin Luther King"! You speak the King's English!

I learned many valuable lessons such as compassion, forgiveness, gratitude and non-judgment. Because of all of these teachings, I never jump to conclusions or assume anything. I never accuse anyone of anything unless I have the facts. I also hold people accountable for their actions. I believe that what you put into the universe comes back to you in one form or another, whether it is positive or negative.

I was taught to love the African Diaspora, our diversity, our skin and hair. They said love your people, though some or all may pull you down like crabs in a bucket, still I love your people. I came from a tribe of strong fierce African Women. If they had not survived the middle passage and slavery, I would not exist!

My spiritual Grandparents taught me that Jesus/Yeshua was of African Descent. I learned that the Roman Emperor Constantine created Christendom/Christianity in 325 A.D. at the council of Nice. Emperor Constantine left out many valuable facts! Jesus and the Madonna were of African Descent, with dark bronze skin, and hair like sheep's wool, and Christianity was built on the symbols, beliefs, and stories of Ancient African/Egyptian Culture! I Images of the Madonna and child are actually taken from images of Isis holding Horus who was born of Immaculate Conception! The greatest artisans were commissioned to paint the face of the Great White Messiah! Leonardo Da Vinci, Michelangelo, Raphael and others were commissioned.

The goal was not to show the Black faced Madonna and child in their Black skin. That was too empowering and too affirming! Jesus, the Christ, was not a Christian at all. Christianity became a tool to divide, conquer, and justify their belief that the whites were superior to all races and cultures. They mislead the world, claiming that they were made in the physical image and likeness of God and Jesus. This religion was used to rationalize the taking of land, culture, family, language and our spiritual beliefs. Because of this 'false teaching' the Africans were reprogrammed, and convinced they were inferior and not quite human!

My Grandmother said, people may dislike or even hate me because I was different.

She went through a list of women in our family who were "different'. She spoke of the hate they experienced in the 70's, and how hard it was, and she did not want any of this to rob me of my right of passage. She instilled in me that we are superior in every way imaginable. This early teaching led me to Theology, Anthropology, Archeology, and of course Egyptology. It gave me the confidence to be myself!

As I grew into adulthood, Biblical based homophobia was always staring me in the face. Homophobia was everywhere! My brother Dijan and I were constantly being verbally accosted by the church, the family, and society in general. People happily used religion and the Bible as a tool to outcast anyone that was different. I think it is so unfair that even today our government uses unfounded religious beliefs to deny SGL/LGBT people our basic rights. It's always been used to dehumanize any group of marginalized people, but I cannot be swayed. I stand on the truth of spiritual laws.

All my life, many in my family found reasons to be homophobic. I was every type of bull dagger, dyke you could imagine! I have been reminded over and over that I am not doing the will of God, God hates homosexuals, and that I'm going to HELL! I told them as I tell everyone, "God does not make mistakes!" God does not see race, religion, sexual orientation, borders of countries, sex, hair texture, eye color, etc! God sees my intentions! God knows my heart, my soul, and my willingness to be of service to others. God sees that I am compassionate, forgiving, and that I love all unconditionally as Jesus did!

I am so not perfect; I have made so many mistakes in life. I believed in the wrong people and placed my faith in the wrong projects. Now I am in a place where I see different. My outlook and myself love is different. I no longer look to other people or things to validate me. I no longer believe people, good or bad can define my destiny! I learned I had to forgive myself for all the many things I was holding against myself! Then I had to forgive others, all of them!!!! Homophobia is merely someone else's self esteem issue. I feel that forgiveness is the medicine, and karma is the cure. I changed my perception of everything!

Most of my life, I saw how the world treated my beloved brother Dijan. It just killed me to see him bullied, hurt and isolated. He was my 'everything'. I knew I was called to be his voice, his advocate, and his protector. As I became more involved in the community, I realized not only was Dijan a target for hate and discrimination, he was a target for the greatest taboo, AIDS.

During my early twenties, Dijan's boyfriend Jermaine was one of my favorite people! Singer and songwriter Jermaine Stewart was my world, my heart. I loved him! I remember when I watched him dance on Soul Train. I loved it! I was so proud as his career soared with background vocals for Shalamar, and then Boy George. I remember the early 90's sitting in the back of his convertible Jaguar XJS as he and my brother shared a Big Gulp while driving through the parking lot at Los Angeles Black Gay Pride. Sometimes I would watch Jermaine and Dijan dance, Jermaine was so tiny! I was in heaven!!!! Just the other day I heard one of his hits on the radio, "The Word is Out"! Hearing it made me sad. My wonderful silly and talented friend/brother in-law died of AIDS March 17, 1997. He was 39.

Dijan like Jermaine was beautiful, silly, poetic, warm, passionate and very creative. He loved to dance, he was my sunshine! The flip side of my brother's creative spark is that he was isolated. He was so alone, and surrounded by pain. He was very aggressive and manly, but in fear of what people were going to do to him. Dijan was most afraid of what the family thought of him. He said they always made him feel there was something wrong with him or he was not good enough. He was continually made to feel like wasn't man enough or he wasn't hard enough. He was made to feel like an embarrassment, a failure, a disgrace to all who came in his path.

Straight people would call Dijan 'sweet'. I saw him targeted over and over again. I remember people teasing him, yelling that he had sugar in his tank. I always wanted to shield Dijan, so that his emotional and physical wounds would begin to heal. Wounds caused by his caregivers, and a system that was supposed to protect him. I suppose my love was never enough.

Were these two needless deaths caused by the sexual prejudice and discrimination of homophobia, and its byproduct hate? It probably was caused by the way society treated gays.

Homophobia is a devastating virus that dehumanizes, and exiles people. Victims of homophobia are cast out by their loved ones, literally thrown away. The result of this is, the exiled person wants and needs to feel loved and wanted. They need to feel human, feel human touch and compassion. Thus, sexual promiscuity....
I need to feel! The flip side is many abuse drugs to eliminate the pain of not being accepted. Drugs are used to feel numb to

the anguish caused by living ostracized from those they love.

The biggest thing I want the world to know about Dijan is that he was a real man. He was loving and compassionate, but ostracized by everything that is supposed to affirm him. Dijan was exiled by The Department of Children's Social Services, family, the church, community and society as a whole.

After 2000, I noticed a change in him. He was no longer silly or full of laughter. He said he was tired of being called sissy by family members, and tired of being held back by society. He said he was tired of people deliberately trying to humiliate him. He felt outcaste, invisible, voiceless, and unwanted. He said, 'no one loved him, and that he didn't really like himself." It hurt to see him in such pain for so many years. He wouldn't let me in. I insisted that he was not worthless, a sissy or anything that people had imposed upon him, but he couldn't hear me.

The last time I saw Dijan was at a family dinner in November of 2003. At first Dijan absolutely refused to attend. He said he was uncomfortable and tired of hiding himself to make *them* comfortable. When he finally did show up, he was different. His eyes were different. His eyes looked as if he could no longer hide his agony. I just grabbed him and hugged him a hard as I could. In my last few conversations with him, he said he didn't know how to be anything other than who he was, and the world hated him for it! He said, "I am a man regardless of how I love"!

To this day there are still a few people in our family who refused to understand why he was in pain or the magnitude of his pain. They refused to look at the fact that they are the catalyst of Dijan's pain, self-hate and isolation. The fact is, the reaction of the family, his schools, churches, and homophobia itself created a climate of fear, isolation, and powerlessness. I suppose he felt helpless his entire life. I remember years ago, he was beaten up in West Hollywood. A family friend's response was, "well if he wasn't prancing a around like a punk, that wouldn't have happened." I heard so much judgment and condemnation, but no one offered help, encouragement or love.

All my life I have used myself as a tool to educate people concerning the issues of homosexuality, homophobia, and all things that oppress us. I wish I could have saved my beloved Dijan. Ultimately Dijan constantly felt a sense of separation. He felt an internalized homophobia. Consciously or unconsciously Dijan felt unworthy, intern allowing the world to determine his destiny. I believe he suffered a spiritual death long before a physical one. Self sabotage, depression, suicide, HIV/AIDS, alcohol and drug abuse are all completely preventable if the person is shown acceptance, understanding, compassion and love.

I had searched for Dijan for about two years. I found my beloved Dijan on May 11, 2006. Dijan died of AIDS on May 25, 2004 alone at Hollywood Presbyterian Hospital. In The final transcripts he said he knew he was alone, and that he was afraid.

In closing you may ask, why is she writing this and why does this matter?
This is for Dijan, and every other human who has suffered in the wake of homophobic hate. I continue to write and spread the message of prevention, awareness, treatment and the socio-economic circumstances that perpetuate this disease. Bullying, suicide, drug abuse, hopelessness, sexual promiscuity is all a derivative of homophobia! In all of my efforts to save our people, I could not save 'my Dijan'. Maybe by writing this, someone somewhere will get the knowledge and spread it!

I believe racism and homophobia are the ultimate ignorance. Education is our greatest tool to fight this ignorance.

For You My Beloved Prince Dijan.
Azaan Kamau

Homophobia & Heterosexism

Homophobia is a social, cultural, and religious illness that paralyzes society. Homophobia has broken down the essential fabric of family and unconditional love. Because of homophobia people have lost jobs, homes, loved ones, and educational opportunities.

Homophobia is a broad topic that comes in many forms. The worst form is internalized homophobia. It stems from the belief that homosexuality about one's self is sinful or ethically unacceptable. Therefore that individual experiences anger, turned within and toward other homosexual people. Interpersonal homophobia is verbal harassment, discrimination, and physical assault against someone homosexual. Institutional homophobia is when government, hospitals, corporations, schools, your church, and other organizations discriminate against people on the basis of their sexual orientation. This has to end!

Heterosexism is the belief that heterosexuals are superior, and the only normal way of human interaction, whether it's sexual or in general.

Heterosexism is similar to institutional homophobia. Heterosexism is the power structure of churches, hospitals, schools, government, and society as a whole that has the power to write laws, or rules that devalue you, your lifestyle and relationship based on what they perceive as normal! , Everyone is expected to conduct themselves in a way that is deemed culturally and sexually normal or live and behave as heterosexual. It's also described as believing everyone is, or should be heterosexual. If you are not heterosexual, you are automatically seem and treated as inferior.

Heterosexism is often the channel by which the lives of SGL/ are demeaned, creating negative cultural images. Living in such a climate where your sexual orientation is consistently devalued and frequently maligned as abnormal, pathological or just not appropriate for any setting. This just further isolates the SGL/ LGBT community, making It harder to find acceptance in society.

Homophobia is further reinforced by the biased belief that heterosexuality is the only legitimate form of human intimacy. Heterosexism is reinforced again and again in our music, the media, movies, television and now the internet.

Heterosexism is further amplified in our discriminative laws, limited rights for same-sex couples, confirms to the masses...these people are not normal.

Homophobia equals oppression. Homophobia in this society hurts everyone, not only LGBT/SGL people. Heterosexuals who are not homophobic are often pressured into actions outside of their humanity. In another instance heterosexuals who have close LBGT/SGL friends are often looked at as questionable to heterosexual society. Heterosexuals are then labeled bi curious. Homophobia limits the necessity of general communication between co- workers, the church, healthcare workers, and family.

There are millions of Conservatives in this country who believe that Same Gender Love is a chosen sin. They believe Same Gender Love is the ultimate sin that is hated by God. They believe it is an abomination and unnatural and can be changed with reparative therapies. In the past, reparative therapies consisted of psycho aversion therapy, castration, hypnosis and electric shock. They adamantly believe that LGBT/SGL people molest children, even though the statistics state quite the opposite! Statistics consistently prove heterosexual males (pedophiles) molest children, not homosexuals. Homophobia thrives on these negative slanderous beliefs.

This backwards thinking has literally destroyed people's lives! This ignorance has eradicated SGL teachers from the educational system. This ignorance has prevented basic equal rights for SGL people such as the right to marry, obtain benefits, or adopt children. The Conservatives would like to minimize and eliminate accurate portrayal of gays in the media. This is ridicules. They would like to allow discrimination in all employment. They would love to retain and amplify laws that criminalize perceived homosexual behavior.

Homophobia in religious, governmental, and corporate form disseminates hate crimes. It spreads it! Homophobia opens the door to hate. Homophobia basically and clearly says, "It's okay to hurt or mistreat this person...we're doing it"!

It is believed that hate crimes against LGBT/SGL people is deserved because they are breaking the laws of God! This thinking spreads hatred and violence like a virus. It welcomes fear and discrimination. It increases judgment and persecution. It creates dysfunction and separation. This is a twisted consciousness. It makes no sense.

Because of homophobia, LGBT/SGL people don't have rights! LGBT/SGL people cannot make legal, financial, or medical decisions for their partner if needed. In many cases a LGBT/SGL person can be denied permission to visit their partner in the hospital. Another amazing fact is that LGBT/SGL people do not have the automatic right to make funeral arrangements. They do not have the right to assume ownership of property after a partner's transition even of it is jointly owned!

Homophobia and anti-gay rearing is the sole reason LGBT/SGL people are pressured into marrying someone of the opposite sex, thus emerged the Down Low! Societies prejudice and traditional religion has helped escalate and perpetuate an individual's false sense of heterosexuality. This pressure propels the individual into feeling and acting as if they must live a lifestyle that is deemed acceptable and socially moral. They design a life that meets all the requirements. This teaching insists ignore your emotions, needs and happiness based on the demands of the populace.

The truth is homophobia is detrimental to the future of all young people. For decades homophobic views have shattered our youth. I believe parental and peer pressure is a direct cause of premature sexual involvement. All youth are pressured into embracing heterosexual behavior to prove to family, friends and clergy they are normal. Media images, parental attitude, religion, and the educational system all reverberate heterosexuality is the norm. Based on this, our youth engage in heterosexual sex to prove they are normal and to be accepted. If you are outside of what is considered normal you are at risk. You are at risk for depression, drug and alcohol abuse. You are at risk for unplanned, unwanted pregnancies. You are risk for getting and spreading a STD. You are risk for contracting HIV/AIDS. You are at risk for suicide!

The deepest wound created by homophobia is being excluded from your family, condemnation from the church, and discrimination from the school. All of these entities have caused the alarming rate of drug usage, homelessness and suicide among LGBT/SGL people.

One problem is sexual topics are not discussed in African American families. Sex and the subject of sex still remain taboo. Even in my own family! My mother just told me a few weeks ago that my Grandmother didn't teach her anything about her body or about sex! Gay topics are not discussed and are out of the question. Homosexual condemnation, slurs and verbal assaults are the extent of dialogue. This exclusiveness has proven to be a death sentence for many. This is merely another example of how homophobia only hurts this society

Junior high school was quite frightening for me. Everyone loved gay bashing, ridiculing and beating up anyone who was different. I was called boy, dyke, it, queer and a host of other horrible names. It was hard to find acceptance among the faculty and students. It was very hard fitting in and staying in a safe place.

When I was a kid, my loved ones found it hard to accept the woman I was growing into. I was taught, my masculinity and non-attraction to boys would not be tolerated. They didn't hide their disgust and embarrassment. They said I was misguided and I needed Christ. My family insisted I was trapped in some sexual rebellion. I needed therapy, I needed a priest and I needed to act like a lady.

I hated their descriptions, I hated who they thought I was. For a long time I was afraid to be myself, afraid to speak my mind. I was afraid to feel. I hid myself because of the awful things that were said and believed about me. My self-esteem was low, and I had no confidence. I felt shame!

My entire environment created insecurities within me. There was nothing loving about it.

My family knew I was hurting. However they never asked what I felt or why I was hurting. When I tried to communicate with them, they just blew me off. They assumed I was in pain because I hated my homosexuality and that I hated myself! That wasn't it. My pain was NOT the result of my homosexuality. My pain was the result of how I was treated. I just wanted to be valued and loved like everyone else.

I believe that homophobia is a sickness in need of curing. It looks bleak and even hopeless at times, but I believe we can prevent this disease from spreading. The fact is we cannot change ones thinking. What we can do is be an example of inclusiveness, compassion and tolerance while teaching our children. With education, positive enforcement of government, and understanding of those who are different we can eliminate this disease once and for all. Hate, segregation and discrimination are counterproductive. Please, embrace life and end homophobia.

African American Historical Viewpoint

In ancient Africa the homosexuals were revered. They were the medicine man, healers and shamans.

It is clearly Western thinking, colonization that has the modern African loathing homosexuals and assumed homosexual acts.

No form of effeminate, femininity, soft or demure nature will ever be tolerated by African America as it pertains to African American Men. No form of Black-Male otherness will ever be accepted or tolerated. African America will never ever accept embrace, tolerate, any Black male that has intimacy with other men.

Any Black man seen as effeminate, soft or not interested in women is automatically called a sissy or a faggot. This person is cast out by his loved ones, exiled by his church and community for embracing White Culture. This person has embarrassed his family, and he his treated as the ultimate abomination. They don't care how pious, religious, spiritual or holy you truly may be. If you walk into a predominantly African American setting, a church, a cookout, a party, or any occasion where African

Americans are congregated, even a little feminine you will receive every ounce of their negative energy. They don't care if you love the Lord. They want you out of their presence! "This person is immoral and has mental illness; this person needs the blood of Jesus!"

No form of dominance, masculinity, hard, rough, athletic, mannish nothing will never ever be accepted by Africa America! No form of African American female otherness will be tolerated. You are reared to clean the house, cook the food, and act and function as a feminine woman. You are taught to stay quiet, and don't have an opinion about anything. It is not at all lady-like to be aggressive toward anything, accept everything as fact, and make yourself look physically appealing to get, keep, and then marry a man. You are encouraged to look and act like a lady to get a husband. I was constantly told, "no man wants a woman that is tougher than him."

Any Black woman seen as masculine, hard, or un-interested in men you were called bull dagger, bull dyke, lesbo and other painful slurs! Let's say I walk into an African American church, they would lose their minds! As I was often told, "there is no place for people like me in the house of the Lord." I would yell back, **"Well My Father's House Has Many Mansions!"**

What is predominantly accepted? Misogyny, hyper-masculine thug society, adultery, burglary, unprotected sex with the opposite sex, car theft, unplanned pregnancies, Black men in and out of jail, rape, physical assault, gang violence, and even murder.

Maybe that's why 70% of African Americans supported Proposition 8! I thought African Americans would be more tolerant, understanding and would never to discriminate against any oppressed people. African Americans have suffered for hundreds of years from all sorts of atrocities. You would think we/ they would be more tolerant!!!

It's sad that our own receive us not!

Faith Based War Against Gay Rights

The faith based war against gay rights is truly engrained in misinterpreted Biblical Scripture.

I remember back in early 2004 when Bishop Eddie Long, along with Dr. King's youngest daughter Bernice King, of all people, led a march to the grave of Dr. King. The march was a protest against same-sex marriage and in support of a national constitutional amendment to protect marriage "between one man and one woman." Long has been considered one the most homophobic black leaders in the anti-gay movement. I think it is so amazing how he has the power to change the negative landscape of African America by providing, education, jobs, low income housing, and hope, but he insists on focusing on the private sex lives of adults in monogamous relationships. According to recent news reports, he now faces the same persecution he used to persecute gays with.

Bishop Long was also one of the leading supporters of George W. Bush's faith-based initiatives. His ministry received one million dollars in grant money from the U.S. Administration of Children & Families!

Currently Eddie Long's church sits on 250 acres and has more than 25,000 members. The church is a $50 million, 10,000-seat cathedral with more than 40 ministries. Some of those ministries consist of "homosexual cure" programs to recruit gays and lesbians for what he called "Sexual Reorientation" conferences! Long's church also offers an ongoing "Out of the Wilderness" ministry to help convert homosexuals into heterosexuals! Shocking Huh?!

Rev. Bernice King has also created quite a reputation of spewing homophobic hate through the years. The Reigniting the Legacy March only kidnapped Dr. King's legacy and showed the country his dream of a non-discriminative environment was just that...a dream!

Bernice King knowing of her parent's support for the SGL/LGBT community, dishonored Coretta Scott King's civil rights legacy by holding the funeral at Bishop Long's church! This information just blows my mind!

Currently Eddie Long, the anti-gay pulpit bully has been charged with allegedly coercing young men into sexual relationships with him. A fourth lawsuit has been filed against Bishop Eddie Long, alleging he pressured a 17-year-old into a sexual relationship during 2005. With these types of role models, leadership, and social structure what is any African American person to think, do or feel?

Black Men, Homophobia & The Down/Low

The down/low is an African American term used to describe heterosexual African American men who are usually educated, successful, married with children that engage in sexual intimacy with other men. These men view themselves as on the down/Low. The main issue is they do not at all identify as homosexual, bisexual, gay, SGL/ LGBT or anything that has any connection to the gay community. They are not feminine, effeminate, soft, or anything that has to do with stereotypical male homosexuality.

The term the Down/Low describes a man that has sexual interaction with men and women, usually without the woman's knowledge.

Many people think the Down/Low was a new form of bi-sexuality or fear of coming out of the closet. In many instances the Down/Low was a rejection of White Culture, White Gay Culture and its terminology. Anything born of White Culture is a slap in the face to the African American race and community as a whole! It is believed still today that homosexuality is a White Man's perversion! The Down/Low is also a rejection of any culture, thought process, belief, ideology of weakness or inferiority.

African American men on the Down/Low only identify themselves as such....an African American Man or a Black Man.

Many families, wives, and colleagues do not know their husband, father, or brother is on the Down/Low. This puts a family though the shock of infidelity, pain, and ultimately disbelief, because of this infidelity, statistics show heterosexual married African American women across the nation are infected with HIV/AIDS!

So, why does this phenomenon exist? **SHAME!**

These men were taught before they could walk how to be a man. Be tough, thug-like, hard, muscular, fearless, rugged, manly, male, strong, empowered, a provider, a father, a husband and most of all masculine!

You can grow up to be a thief, a rapist, a liar, a wife beater, an adulterer, a bigamist, a child molester, an inmate, be involved in bestiality, a murderer, or a necrophiliac (someone who sleeps with corpses) You could even be a cannibal, just don't be Black, homosexual or bisexual!

By the way, if someone in your family is a cannibal, is sleeping with animals or dead

people; this is the time to seek a psychiatrist, not because that person is in a healthy loving relationship with a same gender adult!

Shame is the culprit! Why is the shame so great that a man is forced to live a Down/Low life in secret? Well as I shared before, from birth he has been indoctrinated on who he is to be, how he is to be, and in some instances which woman he is to marry! From the birth, the average African American male has witnessed, heard, and participated in so much homophobia and hate, it's automatic to feel shame for his own personal and private feelings. He learned to feel shame at home, at grandma's, at the cousin's house, at the family reunion, church, at Bible study, at the revival, at the church picnic, in the choir, at school, on the field trip, in the library, at the cafe, in the locker room, on the dance floor, in the elevator at work, when he listens to the community radio station, or when he saw a billboard! Nothing this man grew up with affirmed his thoughts or his feelings about sex and intimacy. He was programmed and taught with the idea that anything gay is White, sick, pathetic, and not of God!

This is a blatant example of homophobia that is culturally taught as the social norm!

Men of the Cloth: Sexual Predators, Perverts & Child Molesters?

Man of the cloth is a term that represents men of the clergy. Other terminology for men of the cloth, are Preachers, Ministers, Bishops, Pastors, Reverends, Priests and Evangelists. Their specific role is to be a spiritual leader and teacher of a ministry, community, and or a church. Many men of the cloth have been given spiritual and administrative authority or other ministers, congregations, and what is taught in the congregation.

Some men of the cloth are not some poor suffering God-fearing lamb that has accidentally crept off the spiritual path. Some of these people are sexual predators, perverts & child molesters. It's seems that some people in the media are misinformed. Any person in power that uses their influence, their money, their authority to coerce an adult or child to engage in sexual acts is a predator, not a homosexual!

I've even read in the media, it is believed there are ministers who adamantly preach against homosexuality also practice it! I think this is a huge misconception! I think that couldn't be farther from the truth.

These homophobes who preach against homosexuality, SGL/LGBT people are opportunist waiting to manipulate someone they see as vulnerable and powerless...your child!

Acts of power, control, expensive gifts, fear, promises of something and submission have nothing to do with SGL/LGBT people in a loving and committed relationship.

When a person in power uses their affluence to manipulate someone, that person should only be viewed as a liar, a hypocrite, and a predator.

At some point we should look at the staggering statistics over the last fifty years to confirm who is really molesting us, and our children. All of the Cardinals and Bishops on the planet cannot deny the facts.

Instead of the religious zealots and hordes pummeling the planet with anti-gay everything, they should be more focused on the hypocrisy among themselves and the poison in the pews.

HIV/AIDS & The Church

Being silent about AIDS in the African American community is internalized terrorism. It is genocide in its highest form. Our people are suffering and dying at catastrophic proportions. We have known how AIDS is transmitted for many years. We have known how to prevent the spread of AIDS for many years. So why are our people still being infected? Why are our youth being faced with death sentences? Why are so many African American women affected by this preventable disease? Where was the church, our backbone when we needed it?

The African American community has a responsibility to be comprehensive and teach based on truth instead of prejudice speculation. They have a responsibility to all of their followers, not to abandon them or treat them with indifference. For years African American organizations, including churches have been silent on controversial topics that directly affect their people. For example divorce, gang violence, abortion, any type of sex etc. **Silence equals death**. This silence or the belief that's it's a white Gay issue has proved to be detrimental.

We should be encouraged to deal with Issues associated with AIDS is controversial and uncomfortable. However that is no reason to embrace denial, or to close your eyes on your people. Communicate and address difficult issues with simplicity and honesty. This thinking that AIDS is and was a gay disease endangers our youth and future of our race. By maintaining silence and supplying improper information only perpetuates the ignorance.

Now that AIDS is swallowing our race, the position of many is abstinence. The just say no approach. But that is not practical in the real world? In the real world we are faced with insurmountable challenges and incorrigible youth. Abstinence is not the answer. Look at our young Black nation. Look at all of the children as a result of someone's sexual immaturity and irresponsibility. Teach prevention. Teach our people the truth about sex, AIDS, and that no one is excluded. Discuss illicit drug use in the Black community and how AIDS is transmitted through needles. Have open discussions about sex. Teach our people the importance of condoms and dental dams. Discuss why it is a necessity and how to use it properly. Teach our people the truths about SGL/ LGBT culture instead of religious rhetoric and criticism.

Teach the fact that HIV/AIDS is not a 'White gay male disease'. Get people's opinions about life, love, sex, the media, and how they are affected. Ask questions about anything those pertain to our "current" society and culture. Not the society and culture of the people who spoke Aramaic, the Ancient Egyptians, The Sumerians or even the Babylonians. Our current society and culture! Education and information is the answer. Our race is dying because of incorrect or no information.

Do not doom our survival because of this subject's discomfort or Biblical Scripture. Have the courage to ask hard questions and look for solutions. African Americans are at risk for extermination. It's clear that some religious organizations base their beliefs on media stereotypes of homosexual people. They believe that all homosexual people are perverted, sexually promiscuous, and morally depraved.

There are two truths that can combat anything. The first truth is knowledge. With knowledge the possibilities of unification is absolutely infinite. If people were inclined to search for knowledge, they would accept the differences of others. If people were taught to explore different cultures, races there would be no judgment. With knowledge we would have a clear understanding that God loves everyone, not just certain people. The second one is unconditional love. If we could just love everyone in the world, there would be no hate. There would be no oppression or separation. There would be no war. If we loved everyone, we would be inclined to embrace people instead of cast them out. Judgment is not the answer. It just continues the oppressive cycle.

I know my philosophy of knowledge and unconditional love is so basic that it seems inconceivable. I believe our religious leaders, organizations and institutions can combine these essential elements into their thought process. Share the knowledge and save a life. Exclusion equals silence. Silence will equal death. Offer those with HIV/AIDS love, compassion and support.

It is believed by many that HIV/AIDS is God's punishment to homosexuals. Therefore homosexuals are unwarrantedly condemned based on Biblical-Mis-interpretations.

Wasn't it Jesus that said for the followers of God to embrace the sick? He said to care for them and condemn them not.

In the past, when the infected faith-filled church attendee would turn to his/her church home for strength, help and guidance they were ignored. Instead of loving and supporting their sick and shut in church members, they turned the other cheek. The church responded with prejudice, discrimination, judgment, ignorance, and hate! Thousands of the churches faith failed died alone, and in vain!

Dr. Martin Luther King & Coretta Scott King Felt...

"Dr. Martin Luther King Jr. envisioned a world where all people would recognize one another as sisters and brothers in the human family. Throughout his life he advocated compassion for the poor, nonviolence, respect for the dignity of all people and peace for humanity." **Martin Luther King III**

When **Coretta Scott King** was asked about her late husband's feelings on SGL/LGBT people, she said, "I believe his dream included SGL/LGBT Americans of any race. He would be the first to say that those participating in Beck's rally have the right to express their views. But his dream rejected hateful rhetoric and all forms of bigotry or discrimination, whether directed at race, faith, nationality, sexual orientation or political beliefs."

"I still hear people say that I should not be talking about the rights of lesbian and gay people and I should stick to the issue of racial justice... But I hasten to remind them that Martin Luther King, Jr., said, 'Injustice anywhere is a threat to justice everywhere' ... I appeal to everyone who believes in Martin Luther King, Jr.'s dream to make room at the table of brotherhood and sisterhood for lesbian and gay people."

"We are all tied together in a single garment of destiny... I can never be what I ought to be until you are allowed to be what you ought to be," she said, quoting from her husband. "I've always felt that homophobic attitudes and policies were unjust and unworthy of a free society and must be opposed by all Americans who believe in democracy."

"Gays and lesbians stood up for civil rights in Montgomery, Selma, in Albany, Georgia, and St. Augustine, Florida, and many other campaigns of the Civil Rights Movement. Many of these courageous men and women were fighting for my freedom at a time when they could find few voices for their own, and I salute their contributions."

"Gay and lesbian people have families, and their families should have legal protection, whether by marriage or civil union. A constitutional amendment banning same-sex marriages is a form of gay bashing, and it would do nothing at all to protect traditional marriages."

"Homophobia is like racism and anti-Semitism and other forms of bigotry in that it seeks to dehumanize a large group of people, to deny their humanity, their dignity and personhood. This sets the stage for further repression and violence that spread all too easily to victimize the next minority group."

"We have a lot of work to do in our common struggle against bigotry and discrimination. I say 'common struggle,' because I believe very strongly that all forms of bigotry & discrimination are equally wrong and should be opposed by right-thinking Americans everywhere. Freedom from discrimination based on sexual orientation is surely a fundamental human right in any great democracy, as much as freedom from racial, religious, gender, or ethnic discrimination."

"We have to launch a campaign against homophobia in the black community."

Coretta Scott King; leader in the civil rights movement.

The Parent's Role

My experience...well my family blamed me for the bullying! Yep the constant harassment, the shame from name calling and the absolute embarrassment that I suffered at the hands of my peers was blamed on me! I was humiliated from both sides! My family said if you weren't stomping around like a bull-dagger, people wouldn't mess with you! Learn to be lady-like. If you weren't so mannish, the kids would not bother you. Well thank God its October of 2010, and hopefully parents will take a different position!

If your daughter cries when you refuse to buy her the big red Tonka fire truck, she insists on wearing a man's tie to school, or she can throw a football like a torpedo, can be very upsetting for a parent. In some cases your son is just Barbie obsessed! He absolutely demands to be a Barbie Princes for Halloween, or insists on smelling pretty can be extremely horrible or a time for growth and learning. Acceptance, non-judgment and love are the keys! Most parents initially blame themselves. They wonder what they did wrong, what they could have changed. In some cases one parent will blame the other! Then after the shock, a parent will wonder who did this to my child? Why did my child choose this?

Again this is emotional for any parent, but you have to ask yourself if you choose to be heterosexual?

Please understand your child is not sexually perverted, immoral, and your child isn't going to hell! SGL/LBGT, homosexuality is much more about love and connection than sex itself. Biblical scholars have even confirmed that the Bible translators are much more concerned about homosexuality in the Bible, than the people in the actual Bible! Imagine that! Many use the Sodom and Gomorrah speech to get you to hate or exile your child. Why was Sodom and Gomorrah really destroyed? Hmmmm, well the Bible actually states it was inhospitality towards travelers from the desert! Ezek. 16:48-50. Not homosexual behavior!

I'll never ever understand how any parent could throw their child away just because he or she is gay! I find it outrageous! I'm also shocked at how common it still is.

If you suspect your child is gay, news flash....you can't beat it out of them! You can't punish them for it. You can't slur or name call it out of them! You can't isolate or deport them, thinking their gayness will magically go away. You certainly can't hate it out of them. Your hatred toward your child or loved one will only cause pain, suffering and strife!

Guide them; encourage them so that they grow up safe, emotionally and sexually empowered. If you don't, your lack of support or homophobia will be your child's mental and physical death.

Homophobia, Bullying & Suicide Prevention

What is homophobic bullying?

Homophobia and bullying is an act of hate, harassment or animosity toward someone SGL/LGBT or even someone assumed to be gay! This harassment includes jokes, slurs, physical, emotional insulting or degrading comments.
Again, it is the schools responsibility to protect your child during school hours, while the child is on campus. Challenging bullying effectively will improve the safety, happiness and learning performance of students.

Many people have committed suicide as a result of homophobic bullying! Unfortunately many hate crimes start off as bullying. I've even heard adults say, "They're just kids, their just being a bully"!

A hate crime is when individuals become victimized because of their sexual orientation, race, or religion. Hate crimes against SGL/LGBT people only arise because the person responsible for act of hate, disgust, etc is homophobic. These attacks of hate and rage are a direct result of social and cultural homophobic beliefs.

This biased social and cultural ideology allows and amplifies homophobia.

What is America doing about our gay youth being bullied to death?
On September 9, 15-year-old Billy Lucas of Greenburg, Indiana, hung himself after enduring constant taunts from bullies at school. Two weeks later, 13-year-old Asher Brown of Houston shot himself soon after revealing he was gay. On September 27, 13-year-old, Seth Walsh of Tehachapi, California, died after injuries sustained from hanging himself. He was regularly tormented while at school. On September 22 suicide of 18-year-old Rutgers University freshman Tyler Clementi was such a horrible shock, even the media felt compassion! Clementi's roommate, Dharun Ravi, broadcasted video footage over the Internet of Clementi engaged in sexual intimacy with another man. Clementi jumped from The George Washington Bridge that separates New York from New Jersey to his death! The fifth young person to commit suicide in three weeks is Raymond Chase, a student at Johnson & Wales in Providence, Rhode Island, died by hanging himself in his dorm room. All of these young people died unnecessarily.

These young people died because they were bullied, and just couldn't take the pain anymore.

America…..this needs to stop!

Unfortunately our church and political leaders, schools, and government institutions have sent a clear message. Your life or the lives of your children mean nothing! We as SGL/ LGBT youth and people are second class citizens, institutionalized heterosexism and homophobia prevail. It is ultimately up to us to educate others to save our lives and the lives of your young people.

Tools to Fight the Ignorance

The suicide rates among SGL/ LGBT teens are four times the rate of their straight teens. In last few weeks, 5 teenagers committed suicide because of homophobic bullying. SGL/LGBT Teens are twice as likely as their heterosexual peers to be depressed and think about or attempt suicide. This is a fact.

The tools to fight the ignorance of homophobia and bullying are pretty simple in my option. I realize some of this may be redundant, but repetition will drive the point home.

Have an open mind to our diverse humanness and our differences. We are all truly all unique in our own way. Let your child know that you will take his or her concerns seriously and will act accordingly. Get the school involved! Have them form an anti-bullying task force. Make them commit to it! Tell your child the he or she deserves respect and to be treated with common decency. If your child is SGL/LGBT and struggling with acceptance, if he is being bullied or he is shutting down, build his self-esteem! Point out all of your child's achievements, how smart they are, how cute their dimples are, and how much they are loved. Lastly teach children to treat others the way they want to be treated!

All of this very basic information can be applied to any and all situations where homophobia is an issue. It doesn't matter whether your child is 10 or 30, hate is real. Education, acceptance, tolerance, understanding and love will change the landscape of homophobia and stop bullying in its tracks.

The Bottom Line

If it weren't for powerful influential prominent leaders like Bishop Eddie Long, all of the other self-loathing homophobic mega church thumpers, and prejudice politics we wouldn't be mourning the deaths of the millions who have lost their fight with HIV/AIDS. We would not be grieving over the numerous people who died at the hands of some homophobic psycho. If this nation just allowed people to be, without judging those who are different, SGL/LGBT youth would not be turning to drugs or committing suicide to escape the pain.

This climate of hate, political malice, and poison in the pew behavior, has got to stop. This very simple book about homophobia and its toxic power was written in one weekend to help save and educate. I am not a perfect human, and I know I don't have all the answers. However, if we can save even one life, we have done our part.

Azaan Kamau October 18th 2010

VICTIMS OF HOMOPHOBIA, BULLYING AND CRIMES OF HATE

1. On July 3, 2000, in Grant Town, West Virginia, Arthur "J.R." Warren was punched and kicked to death by two teenage boys who reportedly believed Warren had spread a rumor that he and one of the boys, David Allen Parker, had a sexual relationship. Warren's killers ran over his body to disguise the murder as a hit-and-run. Parker pleaded guilty and was sentenced to "life in prison with mercy", making him eligible for parole after 15 years. His accomplice, Jared Wilson, was sentenced to 20 years.
2. On September 22, 2000, Ronald Gay entered a gay bar in Roanoke, Virginia and opened fire on the patrons, killing Danny Overstreet, 43 years old, and severely injuring six others. Ronald said he was angry over what his name now meant, and deeply upset that three of his sons had changed their surname. He claimed that he had been told by God to find and kill lesbians and gay men, describing himself as a "Christian Soldier working for my Lord;" Gay testified in court that "he wished he could have killed more fags," before several of the shooting victims as well as Danny Overstreet's family and friends.

3. On June 16, 2001, Fred Martinez, a transgender and two-spirit student was bludgeoned to death near Cortez, Colorado by 18-year-old Shaun Murphy, who reportedly bragged about attacking a "fag".

4. On June 12, 2002, Philip Walsted, a gay man, was fatally beaten with a baseball bat. According to prosecutors, the neo-Nazi views of Walsted's assailant's, David Higdon, led to what was originally a robbery escalating to murder. Higdon was sentenced to life in prison, plus an additional sentence for robbery.

5. The December 2002 homicide of Nizah Morris, a trans woman in Philadelphia, Pennsylvania.

6. The killing of Gwen Araujo, a trans woman, by at least three men who were charged with committing a hate crime. Two were convicted of murder, the third manslaughter; however, the jury rejected the hate crime enhancement.

7. On May 11, 2003, Sakia Gunn, a 15-year-old lesbian, was murdered in a hate crime in Newark, New Jersey. While waiting for a bus, Gunn and her friends were propositioned by two men. When the girls rejected their advances, declaring themselves to be lesbians, the men attacked them. One of the men, Richard McCullough, fatally stabbed Gunn. In exchange for his pleading guilty to several lesser crimes including aggravated

manslaughter, prosecutors dropped murder charges against McCullough, who was sentenced to 20 years. Shocking!

8. On June 17, 2003, Richie Phillips of Elizabethtown, Kentucky was killed by Joseph Cottrell. His body was later found in a suitcase in Rough River Lake. During his trial, two of Cottrell's relatives testified that he lured Phillips to his death, and killed him because he was gay.

9. On July 23, 2003, Nireah Johnson and Brandie Coleman were shot to death by Paul Moore, when Moore learned after a sexual encounter that Johnson was transgender. Moore then burned his victims' bodies. He was convicted of murder and sentenced to 120 years in prison.

10. On July 31, 2003, 37-year-old Glenn Kopitske was shot and stabbed in the back by 17-year-old Gary Hirte, a straight-A student, star athlete and an Eagle Scout, in Winnebago County, Wisconsin. Prosecutors contended that Hirte murdered Kopitske to see if he could get away with it. Hirte pleaded insanity, claiming he killed Kopitske in a murderous rage after a consensual sexual encounter with the victim, because he felt a homosexual act was "worse than murder". The 'temporary insanity' mitigation plea was not upheld, he was found guilty, and received a life sentence.

12. On July 22, 2004, Scotty Joe Weaver was an 18 year-old murder victim from Bay Minette, Alabama, whose burned and partially decomposed body was discovered a few miles from the mobile home in which he lived. He was beaten, strangled and stabbed numerous times, partially decapitated, and his body was doused in gasoline and set on fire.

13. On October 2, 2004, multiple assailants in Waverly, Ohio, attacked Daniel Fetty, a gay man who was hearing-impaired and homeless. Fetty was beaten, stomped, shoved nude into a garbage bin, impaled with a stick, and left for dead; he succumbed to his injuries the next day. Prosecutors alleged a hate crime. Three men received sentences ranging from seven years to life.

14. On January 28, 2005, Ronnie Antonio Paris, a three-year-old boy living in Tampa, Florida, died due to brain injuries inflicted by his father, Ronnie Paris, Jr. According to his mother and other relatives, Ronnie Paris, Jr., repeatedly slammed his son into walls, slapped the child's head, and beat him because he was concerned the child was gay and would grow up a sissy! Paris was sentenced to thirty years in prison. That is just absolutely mind-blowing!

15. On February 27, 2005, in Santa Fe, New Mexico, 21-year-old James Maestas was assaulted outside a restaurant, then followed to a hotel and beaten

unconscious by men who called him "faggot" during the attack. Although all of his attackers were charged with committing a hate crime, none was sentenced to prison.

16. On March 11, 2005, Jason Gage, an openly gay man, was murdered in his Waterloo, Iowa, apartment by an assailant, Joseph Lawrence, who claimed Gage had made sexual advance to him. Gage was bludgeoned to death with a bottle, and stabbed in the neck, probably post-mortem, with a shard of glass. Lawrence was sentenced to fifty years in prison.

17. On February 2, 2006, 18-year-old Jacob D. Robida entered a bar in New Bedford, Massachusetts, confirmed that it was a gay bar, and then attacked patrons with a hatchet and a handgun, wounding three. He fatally shot himself three days later.

18. On June 10, 2006, Kevin Aviance, a female impressionist, musician, and fashion designer, was robbed and beaten in Manhattan by a group of men who yelled anti-gay slurs at him. Four assailants pleaded guilty and received prison sentences.

19. On July 30, 2006, six men were attacked with baseball bats and knives after leaving the San Diego, California Gay Pride festival. One victim was injured so severely that he had to undergo extensive facial reconstructive surgery. Three men pleaded guilty in connection with the

attacks and received prison sentences. A 15-year-old juvenile also pleaded guilty.

20. On August 18, 2006, an altercation occurred in Manhattan between a man and seven black lesbians from Newark, New Jersey. During the altercation, the man was stabbed. The women claim that they acted in self-defense after he screamed homophobic epithets, spit on them, and pulled one of their weaves off, while he has described the attack as "a hate crime against a straight man."

21. On October 8, 2006, Michael Sandy was attacked by four young heterosexual men who lured him into meeting after chatting online, while they were looking for gay men to rob. He was struck by a car while trying to escape his attackers, and died five days later without regaining consciousness.

22. On February 27, 2007 in Detroit, Michigan, Andrew Anthos, a 72-year-old disabled gay man, was beaten with a lead pipe by a man who was shouting anti-gay slurs at him. Anthos died 10 days later in the hospital.

23. On March 15, 2007, in Wahneta, Florida, Ryan Keith Skipper, a 25 year old gay man was stabbed to death. Four suspects were arrested for the crime. The Sheriff is calling it a hate crime.

24. On May 12, 2007, Roberto Duncanson was murdered in Brooklyn, New York. He was stabbed to death by Omar Willock,

who claimed Duncanson had flirted with him.

25. May 16, 2007, Sean William Kennedy, 20, was walking to his car from Brew's Bar in Greenville, SC when Stephen Andrew Moller, 18, got out of another car and approached Kennedy. Investigators said that Moller made a comment about Kennedy's sexual orientation, and threw a fatal punch because he didn't like the other man's sexual preference.

26. On December 8, 2007, 25-year-old gay man Nathaniel Salerno was attacked by four men on a Metro train in Washington, DC. The men called him "faggot" while they beat him.

27. In February 2008, Duanna Johnson, a transsexual woman, was beaten by a police officer while she was held in the Shelby County Criminal Justice Center in Tennessee. Johnson said the officers reportedly called her a "faggot" and "he-she," before and during the incident. In November 2008, she was found dead in the street, reportedly gunned down by three unknown individuals.

28. On February 12, 2008, Lawrence "Larry" King, a 15 year old junior high school student was shot twice by a classmate at E.O. Green School in Oxnard, California. He was taken off life support after doctors declared him brain dead on February 15th. According to reports, prosecutors have charged a 14-year-old classmate with

premeditated murder with hate-crime and firearm-use enhancements.

29. In Rochester, New York on March 16, 2008, police say Lance Neve was beaten unconscious because Neve was gay. A man attacked Neve at a bar leaving him with a fractured skull, and a broken nose. Jesse Parsons was sentenced to more than five years in prison for the assault.

30. In Baltimore County, Maryland on May 29, 2008, eighteen year old Steven Parrish, a member of the Young Swans subgroup of the Bloods was murdered by Steven T. Hollis III and Juan L. Flythe after they found "gay messages" on his cell phone. They felt having a gay member would make their gang appear weak and that by killing Parrish they could prevent that perception.

31. On June 9, 2008, Jeremy Waggoner, an openly gay hairstylist from Royal Oak, Michigan, was brutally murdered in Detroit. His murder is still unsolved.

32. On July 17, 2008, in Colorado, 18 year old Angie Zapata, a trans woman, was beaten to death two days after meeting Allen Ray Andrade. The case was prosecuted as a hate crime, and Andrade was found guilty of first degree murder on April 22, 2009.

33. September 7, 2008 – Tony Randolph Hunter, 27, and his partner were attacked and beaten near a gay bar in Washington DC. Hunter later died from his injuries on September 18.

34. On September 13, 2008, in Denver, Colorado 26 year old Nima Daivari was attacked by a man who called him "faggot". The police that arrived on the scene refused to make a report of the attack!

35. September 15, 2008 – A Bourbonnais, Illinois elementary school bus driver was charged with leading a homophobic attack on a 10-year old student passenger. The boy was taunted by the driver who then encouraged other students to bully then, beat the child.

36. On November 7, 2008, in Newton, NC the home of openly gay Melvin Whistlehunt was destroyed by arsonists. Investigators found homophobic graffiti spray painted on the back of the house.

37. On November 14, 2008, a 22 year old transgender woman, Lateisha Green, was shot and killed by Dwight DeLee in Syracuse, NY because he **thought** she was gay. DeLee was convicted of first-degree manslaughter as a hate crime on July 17, 2009, and received the maximum sentence of 25 years in state prison. This was only the second time in the nation's history that a person was prosecuted for a hate crime against a transgender person and the first hate crime conviction in New York state. Thank God!

38. On December 7, 2008, Romel Sucuzhanya, a 31 year old straight Ecuadorian and his brother Jose, were

attacked on a Brooklyn, New York street for **appearing** to be gay and for being Latino; they were walking arm-in-arm, which is normal for brothers in their culture. Romel later died from his injuries.

39. On December 12, 2008, in Richmond, California a 28 year old lesbian was kidnapped and gang raped by four men who made homophobic remarks during the attack.

40. On December 27, 2008, in Dayton, Ohio 24-year-old Nathan Runkle was brutally assaulted outside a gay nightclub.

41. On February 15, 2009, in New York City Efosa Agbontaen and Branden McGillvery-Dummett were attacked by four young men with glass bottles and box cutters who used anti-gay slurs during the attack. Agbontaen and McGillvery-Dummett both required emergency room treatment for their injuries.

42. On February 18, 2009, two men were arrested in Stroudsburg, PA for the stabbing death of gay veteran Michael Goucher.

43. On March 14, 2009, a gay couple leaving a Britney Spears concert in Newark, New Jersey were attacked by 15 teenaged males. Josh Kehoe and Bobby Daniel Caldwell were called "faggots" and beaten. Caldwell suffered a broken jaw.

44. On March 23, 2009, in Seaside, Oregon two gay men were attacked and left lying unconscious on a local beach. The men

regained consciousness and were treated at a nearby hospital.

45. On April 6, 2009, Carl Joseph Walker-Hoover, an 11 year old child in Springfield, Massachusetts, hanged himself with an extension cord after being bullied all school year by peers who said "he acted feminine" and was gay.

46. On April 11, 2009, a gay man in Gloucester, Massachusetts was attacked and beaten by as many as six people outside a bar. Justin Goodwin, 36, of Salem suffered a shattered jaw, broken eye socket, broken nose and broken cheekbone!

47. On June 30, 2009, August Provost was found shot to death and his body burned at his guard post on Camp Pendleton. LGBT community leaders "citing military sources initially said that Provost's death was a hate crime." Provost had been repeatedly harassed because of his sexual orientation. Military leaders have since explained that "whatever the investigation concludes, the military's "Don't ask, Don't Tell" policy prevented Provost from seeking help." Family and friends believe he was murdered because he was openly gay. The killer reportedly committed suicide a week later after admitting to the murder. Currently no one has concluded if this was a hate crime. *These forty-seven innocent people are on this list are the result of someone's homophobia!*

Resources for the SGL/LGBT Community

Live Out Loud: Working to Foster Gay Youth Pride
American Civil Liberties Union
GLBT National Helpline
Parents and Friends of Lesbians and Gays
The Trevor Project
American Foundation for Suicide Prevention
Anti-Violence Project
Gay and Lesbian National Youth Talk Line
Call toll-free 1-800-246-PRIDE
GLADD
The Gay and Lesbian Alliance Against Defamation
GLSEN
Kaiser Family Foundation.
Lambda Legal
Lesbian Gay Bi Youth Line
ACLU
National Center for Transgender Equality
Youth Resource

Suicide Prevention Life Line

http://www.suicidepreventionlifeline.org
1-800-273-8255

About The Author

Azaan Kamau is the author of numerous books, and has published at total of 27 books through Glover Lane Publishing and Azaan Kamau Media. Azaan is also a poet and photographer!

For signed copies of Azaan Kamau's books or DVDs' please contact
Media Relations:
azaankamau@gmail.com
gloverlane@gmail.com
http://www.azaankamau.webs.com
http://gloverlanepress.webs.com
http://www.lulu.com/spotlight/azaankamau
http://www.blurb.com/user/store/Azaankamau

Please Visit Azaan's Charities:

http://www.outofthecloset.org
http://www.globalfund.org or http://www.joinred.com
http://www.blackaids.org
http://www.redcross.org
http://www.worldvision.org
http://www.directrelief.org
http://www.heifer.org
http://www.habitat.org
http://www.womenforwomen.org
http://www.spca.org
http://www.hsus.org
http://www.networkforgood.org

www.ingramcontent.com/pod-product-compliance
Lightning Source LLC
Chambersburg PA
CBHW070105100426
42743CB00012B/2653